Exploring
South America
Continents of the World
Geography Series

Author: Michael Kramme, Ph.D.
Consultants: Schyrlet Cameron and Carolyn Craig
Editors: Mary Dieterich and Sarah M. Anderson

COPYRIGHT © 2012 Mark Twain Media, Inc.

ISBN 978-1-58037-633-4

Printing No. CD-404176

Mark Twain Media, Inc., Publishers
Distributed by Carson-Dellosa Publishing LLC

Map Source: Mountain High Maps® Copyright © 1997 Digital Wisdom, Inc.

Visit us at www.carsondellosa.com

Table of Contents

Introduction to the Teacher

Exploring South America is one of the seven books in Mark Twain Media's *Continents of the World Geography Series.* The books are a valuable resource for any classroom. This series can be used to supplement the middle-school geography and social studies curriculum. The books support the goal of the National Geography Standards to prepare students for life in a global community by strengthening geographical literacy.

The intent of the *Continents of the World Geography Series* is to help students better understand the world around them through the study of geography. Each book focuses on one continent. Information and facts are presented in an easy-to-read and easy-to-understand format that does not overwhelm the learner. The text presents only the most important information in small, organized bites to make it easier for students to comprehend. Vocabulary words are boldfaced in the text. For quick reference, these words are listed in a glossary at the back of the book.

The series is specifically designed to facilitate planning for the diverse learning styles and skill levels of middle-school students. Each book is divided into several units. Each unit provides the teacher with alternative methods of instruction.

Unit Features
- Close-Up introduces facts and information as a reading exercise.
- Knowledge Check assesses student understanding of the reading exercise using selected response and constructed response questioning strategies.
- Map Follow-Up provides opportunities for students to report information from a spatial perspective.
- Explore allows students to expand learning by participating in high-interest, hands-on activities.
- Glossary lists the boldfaced words with definitions.

Online Resources
- Reluctant Reader Text: A modified version of the reading exercise pages can be downloaded from the website at www.carsondellosa.com. In the Search box, enter the product code CD-404176. When you reach the *Exploring South America* product page, click the icon for the Reluctant Reader Text download.
- The readability level of the text has been modified to facilitate struggling readers. The Flesch-Kincaid Readability formula, which is built into Microsoft® Word™ was used to determine the readability level. The formula calculates the number of words, sentences, and paragraphs in each selection to produce a reading level.

Additional Resources
Classroom Decoratives: The *Seven Continents of the World* and *World Landmarks and Locales Topper* bulletin board sets are available through Mark Twain Media/Carson-Dellosa Publishing LLC. These classroom decoratives visually reinforce geography lessons found in the *Continents of the World Geography Series* in an interesting and attention-grabbing way.

The Continents: Close-Up

A **continent** is a large landmass completely or mostly surrounded by water. The continents make up just over 29 percent of the earth's surface. They occupy about 57,100,000 square miles (148,000,000 sq. km). More than 65 percent of the land area is in the Northern Hemisphere.

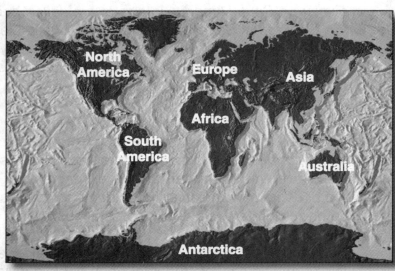

The Continents Today

Landmasses

- Continents: Geographers list North America, South America, Europe, Asia, Africa, Australia, and Antarctica as continents.
- Subcontinents: Greenland and the India-Pakistan area are sometimes referred to as "subcontinents."
- Microcontinents: Madagascar and the Seychelles Islands are often called "microcontinents."
- Oceania: The island groups in the Pacific Ocean are called Oceania, but they are not considered a continent.

How Were the Continents Formed?

For many years, Europeans believed the continents were formed by a catastrophe or series of catastrophes, such as floods, earthquakes, and volcanoes. In 1596, a Dutch mapmaker, Abraham Ortelius, noted that the Americas' eastern coasts and the western coasts of Europe and Africa looked as if they fit together. He proposed that once they had been joined but later were torn apart.

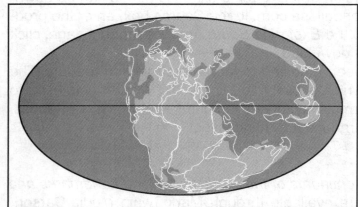

Wegener's theoretical continent, Pangaea, during the Permian Age (white outlines indicate current continents)

Many years later, a German named Alfred Lothar Wegener published a book in which he explained his theory of the "**Continental Drift**." Wegener, like Ortelius, believed that the earth originally had one supercontinent. He named it **Pangaea** from the Greek word meaning "all lands." He believed that the large landmass was a lighter rock that floated on a heavier rock, like ice floats on water.

Wegener's theory stated that the landmasses were still moving at a rate of about one yard each century. Wegener believed that Pangaea existed in the Permian Age. Then

Pangaea slowly divided into two continents, the upper part, **Laurasia**, and the lower, **Gondwanaland**, during the Triassic Age.

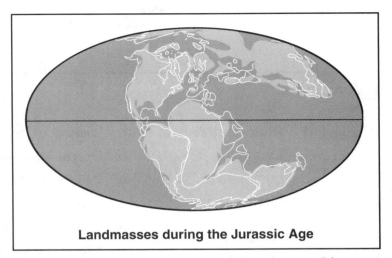

Landmasses during the Jurassic Age

By the Jurassic Age, the landmasses had moved into what we could recognize as the seven continents, although they were still located near each other. Eventually, the continents "drifted" to their present locations.

Most scientists had been in agreement on the continental drift theory until researchers in the 1960s discovered several major mountain ranges on the ocean floor. These mountains suggested that the earth's crust consists of about 20 slabs or **plates**.

These discoveries led to a new theory, "**Plate Tectonics**," which has become more popular. This theory suggests that these plates move a few inches each year. In some places the plates are moving apart, while in others, the plates are colliding or scraping against each other.

Scientists also discovered that most volcanoes and earthquakes occur along the boundaries of the various plates. Recent earthquakes near Indonesia and Japan along the boundaries of the Indo-Australian, Eurasian, Philippine, and Pacific Plates have triggered devastating tsunamis that killed hundreds of thousands of people. Scientists hope that further study will help them increase their understanding of Earth's story.

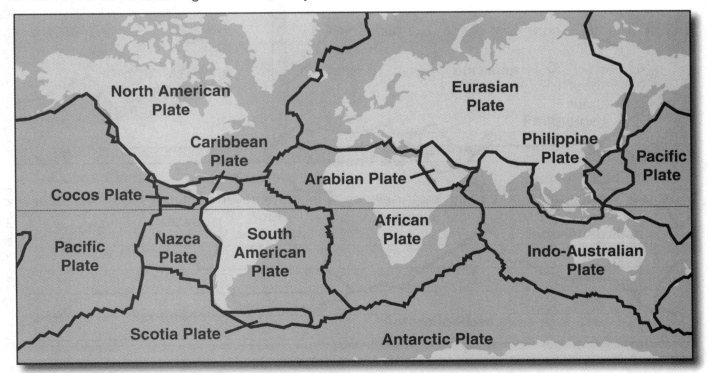

The earth's crust consists of about 20 plates. Plate tectonics suggest that these plates move a few inches each year.

Name: _____   Date: _____

Knowledge Check

Matching

_____   1. Plate Tectonics
_____   2. Laurasia
_____   3. continent
_____   4. Gondwanaland
_____   5. Pangaea

a. lower part of Pangaea
b. Greek word meaning "all lands"
c. theory suggesting that plates move a few inches each year
d. upper part of Pangaea
e. a large landmass completely or mostly surrounded by water

Multiple Choice

6. He explained his theory of the Continental Drift.

    a. Abraham Ortelius
    b. Alfred Lothar Wegener
    c. Pangaea
    d. Laurasia

7. The earth's crust consists of _____ plates.

    a. about 20
    b. about 10
    c. about 5
    d. about 50

Did You Know?

Earth is thought to be the only planet in our solar system that has plate tectonics.

Constructed Response

Explain how the movement of the earth's plates formed the seven continents. Use two details from the selection to support your answer.

_____

_____

_____

_____

_____

Name: _____ Date: _____

Map Follow-Up

Directions: There are seven continents and four oceans. Match the numbers on the map with the names of the continents and oceans.

_____ Pacific Ocean   _____ Arctic Ocean   _____ Atlantic Ocean

_____ Indian Ocean   _____ Africa   _____ Antarctica

_____ Asia   _____ Australia   _____ Europe

_____ North America   _____ South America

Continents and Oceans

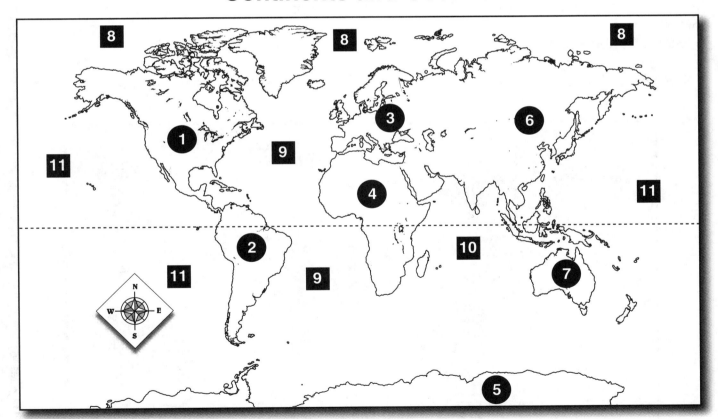

Name: _____   Date: _____

Explore: Continents in Clay

Materials

modeling clay (variety of colors)	poster board	scissors
markers	outline map of continents	

Directions:

Step 1: Cut out the continents from the outline map.

Step 2: Arrange the continents on the poster board.

Step 3: Trace around each continent to create an outline on the poster board.

Step 4: Place a lump of clay on one of the continents. Flatten and mold the clay to fill the outline. Repeat for each of the remaining continents.

Step 5: Label each ocean.

Step 6: On the poster board, write the name of each continent next to its clay outline

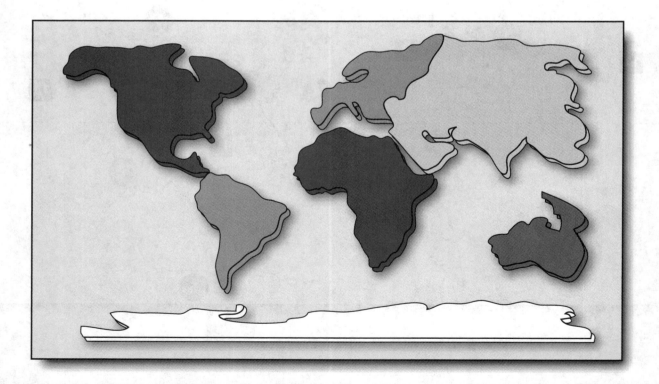

The Continent of South America: Close-Up

South America is the fourth-largest of the seven continents. It covers about 6,880,800 square miles (17,821,000 sq. km). It is almost 4,600 miles (7,400 km) long and about 3,200 miles (5,100 km) across at its widest point.

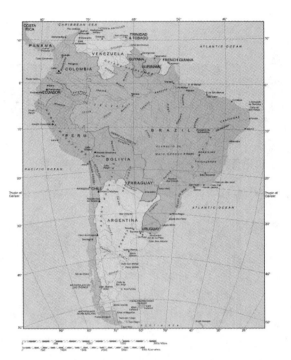

Most of South America is south of the equator. The Tropic of Capricorn nearly bisects the continent. Not only is the continent south of North America, but most of it lies farther east also. Lima, Peru, is one of South America's most western cities. Yet it is farther east than Miami, Florida.

To the north, the continent is connected to Central and North America at the Isthmus of Panama. The northern border is on the Caribbean Sea and the Atlantic Ocean. The eastern border is on the Atlantic Ocean, and the western border is on the Pacific Ocean. South America has many large plains and plateaus. These flatlands are used for farming and raising animal herds. The pampas is a fertile plain used by both farmers and ranchers. South America has some desert land as well.

Rain Forest
- The continent is also known for its vast rain forest areas, especially along the Amazon River basin. Ecologists are concerned about the large areas of rain forest lost each year to development.

Rivers, Lakes, and Waterfalls
- The **Amazon** is South America's longest river and the world's second-longest river. It begins in the Andes Mountains of Peru and travels 4,050 miles (6,518 km) before it empties into the Atlantic Ocean on Brazil's coastline. Although it is not the world's longest river, the Amazon has more tributaries (other rivers and streams draining into it), drains more land, and has a greater volume of water than any other river. Other major South American rivers include the Paraná, Paraguay, and Uruguay Rivers.
- South America does not have many large lakes. Maracaibo is the continent's largest lake. It covers over 6,300 square miles (16,300 sq. km). **Titicaca** is the world's highest navigable lake at an altitude of 12,500 feet (3,810 m). It is in the Andes on the border between Peru and Bolivia.
- South America has many spectacular waterfalls. **Angel Falls** in Argentina is the world's highest waterfall.

Mountains
- The Andes make up the world's longest mountain range. The range stretches about 4,500 miles (7,240 km) along the entire western side of South America. Many of the Andes peaks are over 20,000 feet (6,096 m) high. Only the Himalayas of Asia are higher.
- **Aconcagua**, in Argentina, is the Western Hemisphere's highest point. It is over 22,800 feet (6,950 m) above sea level.

Name: _____ Date: _____

Outline Map of South America

Name: _____   Date: _____

Knowledge Check

Matching

_____ 1. Angel Falls
_____ 2. Amazon
_____ 3. Titicaca
_____ 4. South America
_____ 5. Aconcagua

a. fourth-largest continent
b. Western Hemisphere's highest point
c. world's highest waterfall
d. South America's longest river
e. world's highest navigable lake

Multiple Choice

6. What bisects South America?

a. equator
b. Tropic of Capricorn
c. Angel Falls
d. Atlantic Ocean

7. What connects South America to Central and North America?

a. Isthmus of Panama
b. Tropic of Capricorn
c. Amazon River
d. Maracaibo

Did You Know?

La Paz, Bolivia's capital, is the world's highest capital city. It is 12,000 feet (3,658 m) above sea level.

Constructed Response

South America has many large plains and plateaus. What is this land used for? Use details from the reading to support your answer.

_____
_____
_____
_____
_____
_____
_____
_____

Map Follow-Up

Directions: Match the names listed below with the numbers on the map.

_____ Brazil   _____ Paraguay   _____ Uruguay   _____ Argentina

_____ Chile   _____ Educator   _____ Bolivia   _____ Atlantic Ocean

_____ Colombia   _____ Venezuela   _____ Guyana   _____ French Guiana

_____ Suriname   _____ Cape Horn   _____ Peru   _____ Pacific Ocean

Nations of South America

Name: _____   Date: _____

Map Follow-Up

Directions: Some of the major rivers and lakes of South America are numbered on the map below. Match the numbers on the map with the names listed below.

_____ Paraná River   _____ Tocantins River   _____ Paraguay River   _____ Madeira River

_____ Tapajós River   _____ Xingu River   _____ Amazon River   _____ Negro River

_____ Magdalena River   _____ Orinoco River   _____ São Francisco River

_____ Lake Titicaca   _____ Lake Maracaibo   _____ Lake Poopó

Major Rivers and Lakes of South America

Name: _____ Date: _____

Explore: Folded Booklet

Directions: Research one of the countries of South America. Create the folded booklet below. Organize your information and write it on the pages of the booklet. On several pages, glue magazine pictures, computer-generated graphics, or sketch your own pictures to add color and interest.

Step 1: Fold an 8 1/2″ X 11″ sheet of white paper to make eight sections. Number the sections as shown.	Step 2: Fold the paper in half and cut as shown.	Step 3: Unfold the paper.
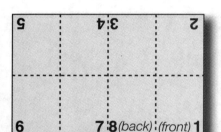	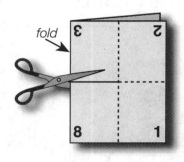	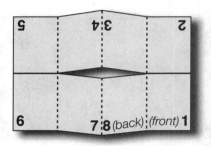
Step 4: Fold the sheet in half, lengthwise, again. Holding one end of the folded page with each hand, lengthwise with the fold at the top, gently push the ends toward the middle. The center sections should move away from each other to form two separate page folds.	Step 5: Fold the sections together so that page 1 is your outer front page and 8 is the outer back page. Flatten all the folds.	Step 6: Now organize your information on the pages of your book. Add illustrations. On one page draw and color the flag of your country. Title your booklet and place your name on the back of the booklet.
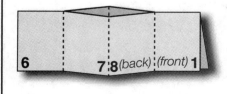	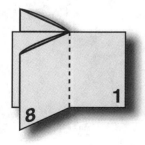	

South America's Climate: Close-Up

South America has a variety of climates. However, because of its location near the equator and the Tropic of Capricorn, the majority of the continent has warm to hot tropical climates. South of the Tropic of Capricorn are more moderate temperatures. This region has cool to cold winters and cool to warm summers.

Trade winds in the Southern Hemisphere blow from the southeast. Moisture from these winds is not blocked until it reaches the Andes Mountains, so much of the continent receives large amounts of moisture.

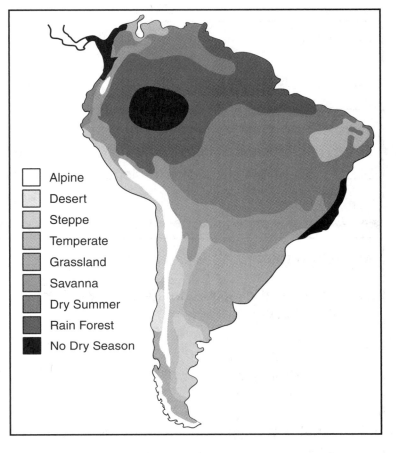

Alpine
Desert
Steppe
Temperate
Grassland
Savanna
Dry Summer
Rain Forest
No Dry Season

Climates of South America

- The region near the equator has a tropical climate. **Tropical climates** have hot temperatures and heavy rainfalls. Most of the Amazon River basin and South America's rain forests are in this region.

- **Humid subtropical regions** (also called **savannas**) of South America lie to the north and south of the tropical region. They include most of central and southern Brazil. In a subtropical region, rain falls on most days in the summer, but the region has a dry season during the winter months.

- **Desert climates** of South America are located in parts of Argentina and along the coast of Peru and Chile. The **Atacama Desert** on the border between Peru and Chile is one of the world's driest places.

- The highlands of South America and the Caribbean and Pacific coastal areas have a **steppe**, or semiarid, **climate**. These regions have hot summers, cold winters, and little rainfall. The largest steppe climate in South America is in Argentina.

- Central Chile has a **Mediterranean climate**. It has warm and dry summers and mild and wet winters.

- Farther south, Chile's climate becomes what is known as a **marine climate**. The marine climate has milder summers than the Mediterranean climate and rainfall occurs year round.

- **Highland climates** are found in the Andes Mountains of Colombia, Ecuador, Peru, Bolivia, Argentina, and Chile. The temperatures vary according to the altitude of the region. The higher the altitude, the colder the temperatures become. Snow is common in the higher altitudes

Name: _____ Date: _____

Knowledge Check

Matching

_____ 1. Mediterranean climate

_____ 2. Atacama Desert

_____ 3. steppe climate

_____ 4. tropical climate

_____ 5. humid subtropical regions

a. warm and dry summers and mild and wet winters

b. savanna climate

c. the world's driest place

d. hot summers, cold winters, little rainfall

e. hot temperatures and heavy rainfalls

Multiple Choice

6. From what direction do the trade winds of South America blow?

    a. northeast
    b. southwest
    c. southeast
    d. northwest

7. What is the type of climate of the Amazon River basin?

    a. humid subtropical
    b. steppe
    c. marine
    d. tropical

Did You Know?

In some parts of South America's Atacama Desert, no rainfall has ever been recorded. This is a satellite view of the desert.

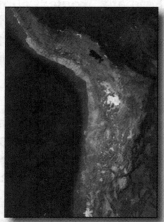

Constructed Response

Explain the difference between a Mediterranean climate and a marine climate. Use details from the selection to support your answer.

_____

_____

_____

_____

_____

_____

_____

Name: _____ Date: _____

Map Follow-Up

Directions: Complete the climate map of South America. Locate and color each of the climate regions on the map. Fill in the Map Key with the colors you used on the map.

Climate Map of South America

Map Key

	Mediterranean Climate
	Savanna Climate
	Steppe Climate
	Desert Climate
	Highland Climate
	Marine Climate
	Tropical Climate

Name: _____ Date: _____

Explore: Climate Regions of South America

Materials

white, unlined paper   scissors
pencil   reading selection

Directions:

Step 1: Fold a sheet of white unlined paper in half like a hotdog bun.

Step 2: Next, turn the paper and fold it into fourths.

Step 3: Unfold the paper. You now have a hotdog folded in 4 equal parts.

Step 4: Cut up each of the folds, making four flaps.

Step 5: On the front of each flap, write the name of one of these climate regions found in the reading selection: tropical climate, savanna climate, steppe climate, and marine climate.

Step 6: Under each flap, write a brief description of the climate region. Write the name of a South American country found within the climate region.

Step 7: Use the foldable to review South America's climate regions.

South America's Resources and Industries: Close-Up

South America has a wide variety of industries and natural resources; however, there are still vast regions that have remained undeveloped. Most of its resources are used for local consumption.

South America's major industry is the processing of **agricultural** products. Other industries important to the economy include the processing of minerals and petroleum. South America is a major world exporter of coffee, copper, bauxite, fish meal, oil seed, petroleum, and petroleum products.

Coffee Berries

Minerals
- Rich mineral deposits are located throughout the continent. The **Incas** discovered and mined gold deposits in the Andes Mountains centuries before the arrival of the first Europeans.
- Throughout the centuries, the mountains of Peru and Bolivia have produced silver. More recently discovered minerals include bauxite, copper, iron ore, tin, lead, mercury, and zinc.

Energy Resources
- The use of hydroelectric power is also common throughout the continent. It accounts for about 66 percent of total energy use.
- While South America has few coal deposits, it does have major deposits of petroleum and natural gas. **Argentina** has over half of South America's oil reserves. **Petroleum** and natural gas are major sources of energy. Wood and charcoal provide energy for some of the manufacturing of iron and steel and the refinement of sugar.

Agriculture
- Much of South America's agricultural products remain on the continent. Many farmers in poorer regions raise just enough food for their own needs. Crops such as bananas, coffee, cotton, and sugar are raised to export. Peru and Chile export grapes, asparagus, and potatoes.
- Ranchers raise beef cattle for both home consumption and export.

Forestry
- While **forests** cover over half of South America, the continent has only a small lumber industry. Exports include only a small percent of the continent's wood and wood products production.

Fishing
- South America is almost completely surrounded by oceans, yet it has a small fishing industry. Most commercial fishing is for local consumption. Major fish harvests include anchovies, tuna, and crustaceans such as crabs, lobsters, and shrimp.

Manufacturing
- Important manufacturing products include beverages, electrical and mechanical equipment, motor vehicles, plastics, and textiles.

Name: _____ Date: _____

Knowledge Check

Matching

_____ 1. Argentina

_____ 2. petroleum

_____ 3. Incas

_____ 4. forests

_____ 5. processing agricultural products

a. South America's major industry

b. first mined gold in the Andes Mountains

c. cover over half of South America

d. has most of South America's petroleum reserves

e. one of the major sources of energy

Multiple Choice

6. Which two South American countries have long been a source of silver?

    a. Peru and Chile
    b. Peru and Bolivia
    c. Chile and Brazil
    d. Argentina and Chile

7. What percent of South America's energy is produced by hydroelectric sources?

    a. about 66 percent
    b. about 42 percent
    c. about 70 percent
    d. about 30 percent

Did You Know?

Alcohol made from sugar cane is a major source of automobile fuel in Brazil.

Constructed Response

Explain why South America does not export many agricultural products. Use details from the selection to support your answer.

_____

_____

_____

_____

_____

_____

_____

Name: _____   Date: _____

Map Follow-Up

Directions: Complete the map below. Create a symbol for each of the products and natural resources listed in the Map Key. Draw the symbol in the Map Key. Add the symbol to the blank map to show the region in South America that is a major source of the product or natural resource.

Resources and Products of South America

Map Key

_____ Coal

_____ Coffee

_____ Forestry

_____ Bananas

_____ Gold

_____ Iron Ore

_____ Livestock

_____ Natural Gas

_____ Petroleum

_____ Silver

South America's Animal Life: Close-Up

Spectacled Bear

South America has many common species of animals, but it is the home to many unique ones as well.

Mammals

- Larger mammals are rare in South America. The continent is home to only one type of bear, the **spectacled bear**. Horses were not native to South America but were introduced by early Spanish settlers.
- Some of the more interesting South American mammals include anteaters, armadillos, capybaras, chinchillas, marmosets, opossums, porcupines, sloths, and tapirs. Freshwater dolphins and manatees live in the Amazon.
- The continent also includes varieties of rats, mice, and bats. A unique bloodsucking bat lives on the continent.
- South America is the home to many species of monkey. Howler monkeys and ringtail monkeys are unique to the continent.
- Members of the cat family on the continent include jaguars, ocelots, and pumas.
- The South American llama, alpaca, and vicuña are related to the camel. Because the alpaca and llama are such sure-footed animals, they are an important means of transporting material on the steep slopes of the Andes Mountains. They also supply the people with meat, milk, and wool.

Fish

- South America is home to many varieties of freshwater fish. The **piranha**, a flesh-eating fish, is common in jungle waters. Other unusual species include flying fish and electric eels.

Birds

- Over 2,700 species of birds live in South America. Flamingos, hawks, macaws, parrots, and parakeets inhabit the tropic regions. The harpy eagle is one of South America's more rare birds. The Humboldt penguin lives along some of the southern coastal areas. The largest flightless bird on the continent is the **rhea**, which is related to the ostrich. The largest bird capable of flight is the **condor**. Andean condors often have wingspans of over ten feet (3 m) and can fly at altitudes of over 25,000 feet (7,620 m).

Reptiles

- A variety of reptiles lives in the jungle regions of South America. Boas, **anacondas**, iguanas, caimans, and crocodiles are found in many areas. The anaconda is the world's largest snake. It is a type of boa, sometimes growing to over 20 feet (6 m) in length.

Galápagos Islands

The Galápagos Islands, located off the coast of Ecuador, are home to unique animals including Darwin finches, the Galápagos penguin, and the Galápagos tortoise. The Galápagos tortoise often grows to a weight of over 500 pounds (189 kg), and many live over 100 years.

Galápagos Tortoise

Name: _____   Date: _____

Knowledge Check

Matching

_____ 1. anaconda

_____ 2. spectacled bear

_____ 3. piranha

_____ 4. condor

_____ 5. rhea

a. South America's largest flightless bird

b. world's largest snake

c. only type of bear native to South America

d. South America's largest flying bird

e. South American flesh-eating fish

Multiple Choice

6. What South American animal sometimes lives over 100 years?

   a. Galápagos tortoise
   b. Darwin finches
   c. iguanas
   d. flamingos

7. What two types of monkeys are unique to South America?

   a. vicuña and piranha
   b. rhea and condor
   c. caiman and capybaras
   d. howler and ringtail

Did You Know?

The back talons of the harpy eagle can be as big as grizzly bear claws. Harpy eagles eat mostly animals that live in the trees of the tropical forest, like sloths, monkeys, and opossums.

Constructed Response

Explain why llamas are so important to the people of the Andes. Use at least two details from the selection to support your answer.

_____

_____

_____

_____

_____

_____

The People of South America: Close-Up

South America has a variety of ethnic groups. Major groups include Native Americans as well as descendants of Spanish and Portuguese settlers and African slaves. Through the years, much mixing of the ethnic groups occurred. **Mestizo** is the name given to a large part of the population who are descended from the Native Americans, the Spanish, and the Portuguese.

Quechua Woman and Child of Peru

Many of South America's natives are descendants of the ancient Inca civilization. The Incas lived mainly in the Andes Mountains. The Inca civilization flourished before the arrival of the Europeans. They had major cities and a road system of over 12,000 miles (19,312 km). They developed terrace farming and created large irrigation systems.

In the 1500s, Spanish soldiers, called **conquistadors**, conquered much of the continent. The Conquistadors came in search of gold and other riches. They enslaved much of the native population and also brought slaves from Africa to work in the mines. The South American countries continued to be colonies of European nations until they achieved independence beginning in the early 1800s. The last nations to win independence were Guyana (British Guiana) in 1966 and Suriname (Dutch Guiana) in 1975.

Today, most of the Native Americans live in the highlands of the Andes Mountains. Spanish descendants are common in Argentina and Uruguay. Portuguese descendants are most common in Brazil. Many immigrants from other European countries later joined the early Spanish and Portuguese settlers.

Population

Street Market in Brazil

South America's population continues to increase at a rapid rate. The population doubled between 1960 and 2000. Nearly one-half of the total population lives in Brazil. Migration from the rural areas to cities continues to increase. In many of the South American countries, the urban population is over 80 percent. Most of South America's people live near the coasts, and very few inhabit the large central area of the continent.

Language

Spanish is the official language of most of the continent, while **Portuguese** is the official language of Brazil. Other official languages include English in Guyana, Dutch in Suriname, and French in French Guiana. Many native languages are still spoken in the highlands of Bolivia, Chile, Paraguay, and Peru.

Religion

About 85 percent of the population of South America is **Roman Catholic**. Members of both the Protestant and Jewish faiths also live throughout the continent.

Name: _____ Date: _____

Knowledge Check

Matching

____ 1. mestizo

____ 2. conquistadors

____ 3. Portuguese

____ 4. Spanish

____ 5. Roman Catholic

a. official language of Brazil

b. South America's largest religious group

c. official language of most of South America

d. descended from Native Americans and Spanish and Portuguese settlers

e. Spanish soldiers

Multiple Choice

6. What ancient Native American civilization flourished in the Andes?

    a. Spanish

    b. Portuguese

    c. Mayan

    d. Inca

7. In which country does nearly one-half of South America's population live?

    a. Chile

    b. Brazil

    c. Argentina

    d. Peru

Did You Know?

The population of South America is about 386 million. This is about six percent of the world's population.

Constructed Response

What effect did the Spanish Conquistadors have on the continent of South America? Use details from the selection to support your answer.

_____

_____

_____

_____

_____

_____

_____

The Inca Civilization: Close-Up

The early history of the Incas is a mystery. Since the Incas never developed a system of writing, we must rely on the writings of their **Spanish** conquerors for any early Inca history. We can also study artifacts of the ancient cities for clues to the early Incas' story.

We do know some Inca myths. One early story is that the sun god created the first Inca, **Manco Capac**, and his sister. The god told them to go and teach other Indians. They went into the wilderness to establish a city. They named their city **Cuzco**, and it became the capital of the Inca Empire.

The Incas probably began as one of the many small tribes of the Andes Mountains. At its peak, the Inca Empire spread through parts of what are now Peru, Ecuador, Chile, Bolivia, and Argentina. The Inca land included desert, fertile valleys, some rain forests, and the Andes Mountains.

The Incas conquered most of their territory under the leadership of Pachacutec, who ruled from 1438 to 1471. The Incas crushed most of the other tribes during brutal fighting.

Machu Picchu

The Inca Empire was so large that a system of roads was built that stretched over 12,000 miles (19,312 km). The Incas did not use wheeled vehicles on their roads. The great road system was for pedestrians. Only the road system of the ancient Romans was equal to that of the Incas.

Interesting Facts

- The Incas developed terrace farming. They cut terraces into the steep sides of the mountains to create more farmland. They also dug irrigation systems to bring water from the mountain streams to the terraces. Many of the Inca roads, terraces, and irrigation ditches are still in use today.
- The llama was an important animal for the Incas. They tamed the llama and used it for transportation of people and materials. The llama also provided the Incas with wool and food.
- The Incas developed a counting system that used a base of ten. They used a **quipu** to remember the numbers. The quipu had a main cord about two feet long. Many colored strings were tied to the main cord. Each string had knots tied in it. The color of the strings and the distance between the knots had special meaning.

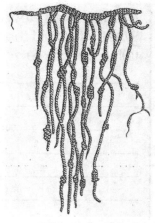

The Inca civilization was at its peak when the Spanish arrived. **Francisco Pizarro** led the Spanish invaders against the Incas. After a series of fierce battles, the Spanish defeated the Inca king, Atahualpa, and in 1533 he was killed. The descendants of the Incas continued to live under the rule of the Spanish until the various countries in which they lived became independent.

Name: _____ Date: _____

Knowledge Check

Matching

_____ 1. Manco Capac

_____ 2. Spanish

_____ 3. Cuzco

_____ 4. quipu

_____ 5. Francisco Pizarro

a. led the Spanish invaders

b. Inca invention used for counting

c. first Inca, according to an Inca myth

d. conquered the Incas

e. capital of the Inca Empire

Multiple Choice

6. Who ruled the Incas from 1438 to 1471?

    a. Pachacutec
    b. Pizarro
    c. Capac
    d. Cuzco

7. What Inca king was killed in 1533 by the Spanish invaders?

    a. Pachacutec
    b. Pizarro
    c. Atahualpa
    d. Capac

Did You Know?

The Incas were the first people to grow potatoes. Spanish explorers introduced the vegetable to Europe.

Constructed Response

Describe two innovative farming methods used by the Incas. Use details from the selection to support your answer.

_____

_____

_____

_____

_____

_____

_____

Name: _____ Date: _____

Map Follow-Up

Directions: The Inca Empire included parts of the countries that are now Peru, Ecuador, Chile, Bolivia, and Argentina. Label those countries on the map below as well as the Caribbean Sea, Atlantic Ocean, and Pacific Ocean.

The Inca Civilization

South American Culture: Close-Up

South American history and culture can be easily divided into three periods: native, colonial, and post-revolutionary.

Native populations lived throughout the continent. The most notable of the many tribes was the Incas of the Andes Mountains. Native arts included beautiful ceramics, textiles, and feather work, as well as gold and jewelry work. The architecture of the ancient times included magnificent structures, such as those in the cities of Cuzco and Machu Piccu.

The **colonial period** began with the Spanish and Portuguese conquests in the sixteenth century. This period is most noted for its architecture and religious art. Many beautiful paintings and stone carvings still adorn the beautiful churches and cathedrals throughout the continent.

Revolutions against the European rule began in the early 1800s. Soon most of South America's nations became independent.

Literature
- In more modern times, literature increased in importance. Many South American authors became internationally famous. Nobel Prize winners include **Pablo Neruda**, Gabriel Garcia Marquez, Mario Vargas Llosa, and Gabriela Mistral.

Festivals
- South America is a land of many festivals. These festivals are a combination of native and colonial, as well as religious celebrations. These festivals feature music, dance, food, and colorful costumes.

Music
- Music has long been an important part of South America's heritage. The native civilizations used a variety of drums and flutes to accompany several festivals. The Europeans introduced stringed instruments to the continent. The **guitar**, introduced by the Spanish, became a favorite instrument. Today's South American music is a blend of native, African, and European influences.

Dance
- Dance has always been part of South American culture. In the twentieth century, several dances from Brazil, such as the maxixe, samba, lambada, and bossa nova, gained international popularity. The **tango** is a popular dance from Argentina.

Language
- **Spanish** is the official language of most of the South American countries. However, about half of the population speaks Portuguese, the official language in Brazil. Other official languages include English in Guyana, Dutch in Suriname, and French in French Guiana. Minorities in many countries also use native languages.

Religion
- About 85 percent of South America's people are Roman Catholic. This number has been dropping in recent years. Spanish and Portuguese conquerors brought the Roman Catholic faith to the continent. Most of the Protestant Christians live in Brazil and Chile. The Jewish population lives mainly in cities throughout the continent.

Name: _____ Date: _____

Knowledge Check

Matching

_____ 1. guitar
_____ 2. colonial period
_____ 3. Spanish
_____ 4. Pablo Neruda
_____ 5. tango

a. name of a popular dance from Argentina
b. Nobel Prize-winning author
c. instrument introduced by the Spanish
d. noted most for its architecture and religious art
e. the official language of most of the South American countries

Multiple Choice

6. Which country was the source of most popular South American dances in the twentieth century?

   a. Peru
   b. Brazil
   c. Suriname
   d. French Guiana

7. Which is NOT one of the main periods of South American history and culture?

   a. native
   b. colonial
   c. post-revolutionary
   d. pre-historic

Did You Know?

One of South America's most famous festivals is Brazil's Carnival. It is celebrated throughout the country beginning on the Saturday before Ash Wednesday.

Constructed Response

Explain how music has been an important part of South America's heritage. Use at least two details from the selection to support your answer.

_____
_____
_____
_____
_____
_____
_____

Brazil, Paraguay, and Uruguay: Close-Up

Brazil

- **Brazil** is South America's largest country. It is also its most populous. Nearly one-half of South America's population lives in Brazil. Most of Brazil's people live within 200 miles of the Atlantic Ocean coastline.
- **São Paulo** is Brazil's largest city. It is the world's seventh-largest city. Brazil's other large cities are Rio de Janeiro, Salvador, and the capital city, **Brasília**.
- Much of the interior of Brazil contains tropical forests. The Amazon River runs through the heart of the country.
- Brazil exports more sugar cane and oranges than any other country. It also produces over one-third of the world's coffee. Other major exports include rubber, cacao, bananas, pineapples, lemons, rice, and cotton.
- Brazil has large deposits of minerals and gemstones. However, it does not have major reserves of oil.

Paraguay

- Paraguay is a landlocked country. However, it contains three major rivers, the Paraguay, the Paraná, and the Pilcomayo. The Paraná flows into the Atlantic Ocean, giving Paraguay a shipping outlet.
- **Asunción** is Paraguay's capital and largest city. It is located where the Paraguay and Pilcomayo rivers meet. The country of Argentina is just across the rivers from Asunción.
- The Paraguay River also divides the country into eastern and western regions. The western region has over three-fifths of Paraguay's land and only five percent of its people. The harsh climate and poor transportation have hindered the development of the region. The eastern region has tropical forests and fertile grasslands. Major products of the region include cattle, coffee, cotton, and tobacco.

Uruguay

- The capital and largest city of Uruguay is **Montevideo**.
- Most of Uruguay's land is grassland. This helps support large herds of cattle and sheep. Most of the nation's industry is related to raising and processing these herds. Meatpacking, wool, and textiles are of great importance to Uruguay's economy.
- Less than ten percent of Uruguay's land is used for farming. Major crops include citrus fruits and grains. Flaxseed is an important crop, used in the manufacture of ink, linseed oil, and paint.
- In recent years, tourism has continued to grow as an important part of Uruguay's economy. Many resorts are on its Atlantic Ocean coastline.

Name: _____ Date: _____

Knowledge Check

Matching

_____ 1. Brasília

_____ 2. São Paulo

_____ 3. Brazil

_____ 4. Montevideo

_____ 5. Asunción

a. Paraguay's capital and largest city

b. South America's largest country

c. Brazil's capital city

d. Brazil's largest city

e. capital and largest city of Uruguay

Multiple Choice

6. Which is NOT a major river in Paraguay?

   a. Pilcomayo
   b. Paraná
   c. Amazon
   d. Paraguay

7. Which is NOT a major export from Brazil?

   a. sugar cane
   b. oranges
   c. beef
   d. bananas

Did You Know?

Most of the Amazon River runs through Brazil. It is both the world's widest and deepest river.

Constructed Response

Why is flaxseed considered an important crop for the country of Uruguay? Use details from the selection to support your answer.

_____

_____

_____

_____

_____

_____

_____

_____

Name: _____   Date: _____

Map Follow-Up

Directions: Match the names listed below with the numbers on the map.

_____ Brazil   _____ Paraguay   _____ Uruguay

_____ Atlantic Ocean   _____ Cape Horn   _____ Pacific Ocean

Nations of Brazil, Paraguay, and Uruguay

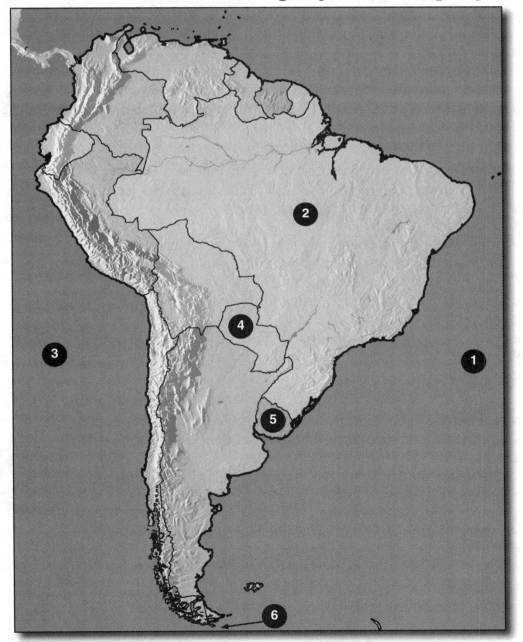

Colombia, Ecuador, and Venezuela: Close-Up

Colombia

- Colombia became independent from Spain in 1819. **Bogotá** is Colombia's capital and major industrial city.
- Colombia's major industries include farming and mining. Petroleum accounts for about 40 percent of Colombia's export income.
- **Colombia** has the world's largest deposits of platinum. It also has major deposits of gold and emeralds. It supplies about 90 percent of the world's emeralds.
- Coffee, cotton, corn, rice, potatoes, and sugar cane are major crops. Coffee once accounted for about 80 percent of Colombia's export income. That is now down to about 10 percent. Flowers are also raised for export.

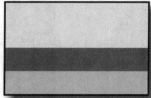

Ecuador

- Ecuador was once the northern part of the ancient Inca Empire. The Spanish conquered the region in 1533. Ecuador gained independence in 1822 and became part of Colombia.
- It separated from Colombia in 1830.
- The **Andes Mountains** cover about one-fourth of Ecuador's land area. The mountain region contains many mineral resources and is the site of much tourism. **Quito**, Ecuador's capital, is located in the Andes foothills.
- The coastal plain contains rich farmland. Major crops grown for export include bananas, cacao, and coffee.
- The eastern region of Ecuador contains tropical jungles. It is poorly developed. Deposits of petroleum were discovered in the 1960s, and today, petroleum accounts for about half of Ecuador's exports.

Venezuela

- Venezuela has been a major producer of petroleum since the 1920s. Today, petroleum accounts for 95 percent of the nation's export income.
- Venezuela's capital, **Caracas**, has many beautiful skyscrapers and homes. However, there are also major slum areas where people suffer from malnutrition and extreme poverty.

- Raising cattle has been important to Venezuela's economy for many years. Recently, because of irrigation projects, more of the country's land is becoming farmland.
- Mining has also been an important part of Venezuela's economy. Miners have been extracting diamonds and iron ore for many years. Much of the iron ore was shipped to the United States to be made into steel.

Name: _____ Date: _____

Knowledge Check

Matching

_____ 1. Andes Mountains
_____ 2. Caracas
_____ 3. Bogotá
_____ 4. Quito
_____ 5. Colombia

a. Venezuela's capital
b. Ecuador's capital
c. has the world's largest deposits of platinum
d. Colombia's capital
e. covers about one-fourth of Ecuador's land area

Multiple Choice

6. What percent of Venezuela's export income comes from petroleum?

   a. 55 percent
   b. 70 percent
   c. 95 percent
   d. 10 percent

7. Colombia provides 90 percent of the world's supply of what gemstone?

   a. jade
   b. emeralds
   c. diamonds
   d. rubies

Did You Know?

Much of the world's illegal drug supply comes from Colombia. Many nations are working with Colombia to cut down on drug traffic. Cocaine is made from the coca leaf.

Constructed Response

Explain why mining is an important part of Venezuela's economy. Use details from the selection to support your answer.

_____

_____

_____

_____

_____

_____

_____

Name: _____ Date: _____

Map Follow-Up

Directions: Match the names listed below with the numbers on the map.

_____ Colombia   _____ Ecuador   _____ Venezuela

_____ Atlantic Ocean   _____ Caribbean Sea   _____ Pacific Ocean

Nations of Colombia, Ecuador, and Venezuela

Argentina, Chile, Peru, and Bolivia: Close-Up

Argentina

- Argentina came under Spanish control in 1516. In 1816, Spanish colonists gained independence. Buenos Aires is Argentina's capital, largest city, and major port.
- The northern part of Argentina is a subtropical region, the **Chaco**. It is mainly a forest region. Farther south, the **Pampas** grassland contains some of the world's most fertile soil. Livestock including cattle, sheep, and hogs and crops, such as alfalfa, corn, flax, soybeans, and wheat are grown there. **Flax** is used to make linen cloth.
- The southern part of Argentina is a high plain named **Patagonia**. It is a cold, dry, windy, sparsely populated region. The western border with Chile is in the Andes Mountains.

Chile

- Chile is a long, narrow country along the Pacific Ocean coast. The northern region is primarily desert. The **central valley** of Chile has flat land and a mild climate where over three-fourths of the population lives. The Archipelago in the south has few people and little farmland. It is made up of thousands of small islands.
- Chile's capital and largest city is **Santiago**. Santiago, Concepción, and Valparaiso are all becoming major industrial cities.
- Agriculture has long been Chile's major industry, but manufacturing, especially steel, has been increasing in recent years. Agricultural products include corn, potatoes, sugar beets, grapes, and wheat. Chile also has a major wine industry. Cattle, poultry, and sheep make up one-third of Chile's agricultural products.

Peru

- Peru's capital and largest city is **Lima**.
- The country has three major regions: its coastal region, the Andes Mountains, and the plains at the base of the Andes. Peru's coastal waters help support a major fishing industry; anchovies are a major part of each year's fish harvest.
- The Andes contain many valuable minerals, including copper, gold, iron ore, lead, silver, and zinc. The Andes foothills include rain forests and jungles. Many of Peru's native population live in the Andes foothills. In recent years, petroleum has been discovered in the region.

Bolivia

- Bolivia is a landlocked country and has had less outside influence than many of the other South American countries. Much of the country is part of the **Altiplano Plateau** in the Andes, where approximately 40 percent of the population lives. **La Paz** is Bolivia's capital.
- Agriculture is the major industry, with potatoes, wheat, and a plant called **quinoa** grown on the Altiplano and bananas, cacao, coffee, and maize grown in the lowlands.
- Major exports include tin, tungsten, and silver.

Name: _____ Date: _____

Knowledge Check

Matching

_____ 1. Pampas grasslands

_____ 2. Santiago

_____ 3. La Paz

_____ 4. Lima

_____ 5. Chaco

a. Bolivia's capital

b. Peru's capital and largest city

c. Chile's capital and largest city

d. contains some of the world's most fertile soil

e. name of the northern subtropical region of Argentina

Multiple Choice

6. What type of fish is a major part of Peru's annual fish harvest?

   a. salmon
   b. tuna
   c. anchovies
   d. piranha

7. What is the name of the high plain in the southern part of Argentina?

   a. Chaco
   b. Pampas
   c. Patagonia
   d. quinoa

Did You Know?

Mount Aconcagua is the highest peak in the Western Hemisphere. It is located in the Andes Mountains in Argentina.

Constructed Response

Explain the difference between the northern and southern parts of Argentina. Use details from the selection to support your answer.

_____

_____

_____

_____

_____

_____

_____

Name: _____   Date: _____

Map Follow-Up

Directions: Match the names listed below with the numbers on the map.

_____ Argentina   _____ Chile   _____ Peru   _____ Bolivia

_____ Atlantic Ocean   _____ Cape Horn   _____ Pacific Ocean

Nations of Argentina, Chile, Peru, and Bolivia

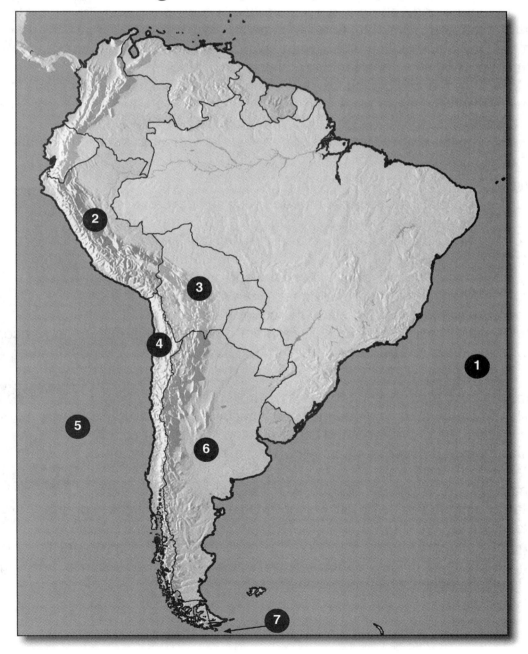

Guyana, French Guiana, and Suriname: Close-Up

The Guianas are two small nations and a colony on the north central Atlantic Ocean coast of South America.

Guyana

- Guyana was first settled by the Dutch in the late 1500s. The British gained control in 1814 and named the colony British Guiana. It became an independent nation and changed its name to Guyana in 1966.
- **Guyana** means "land of many waters." In addition to its Atlantic Ocean coastline, Guyana has many rivers.
- Both the Dutch and British established towns and large plantations. They also imported many slaves from Africa and Asia. Farming and mining are the nation's major industries. Major crops include cacao, coffee, citrus fruits, sugar cane, and rice.
- Guyana is also a source of diamonds, gold, bauxite, and manganese.
- Guyana's capital, **Georgetown**, is on the Atlantic Ocean coast at the mouth of the Demerara River. It was named for England's King George III.

French Guiana

- French Guiana is still a colony of France. French settlers came to the territory in 1604 and claimed it as a colony in 1667. Almost 45 percent of the nation's people live in or near the capital city, **Cayenne**.
- Most of the population of French Guiana is descended from the many slaves imported in early years to work on the plantations. Most of the people live near the coast. However, tribes of Native Americans live in the rain forests of the country's interior.
- French Guiana has rich, fertile soil. Farmers grow bananas, cacao, corn, rice, and sugar cane. Other industries include the mining of gold and the harvesting of timber.

Suriname

- **Suriname** (also spelled Surinam) was controlled alternately by the British and Dutch until it gained independence in 1975. From 1815 until independence, it was named Dutch Guiana. It went from a military to an elected government in 1988. **Paramaribo** is Suriname's capital and only major city.
- Suriname is a mountainous country, so most of its people live along the flat land at the coast. Almost half of the total population lives in or near Paramaribo, the capital city.
- Mining is Suriname's major industry. Ninety percent of its exports are bauxite, aluminum oxide, and aluminum. Major crops include bananas, cacao, coffee, rice, and sugar cane. Its forests also supply lumber and wood products.

Name: _____ Date: _____

Knowledge Check

Matching

_____ 1. Paramaribo
_____ 2. Guyana
_____ 3. Cayenne
_____ 4. Georgetown
_____ 5. Suriname

a. Guyana's capital
b. Suriname's capital
c. Dutch Guiana was this country's name
d. means "land of many waters"
e. capital of French Guiana

Multiple Choice

6. What Europeans first settled in what is now Guyana?

   a. French
   b. German
   c. Dutch
   d. Scandinavians

7. When did French settlers first come to what is now French Guiana?

   a. 1667
   b. 1604
   c. 1975
   d. 1815

Did You Know?

Cayenne is a hot pepper. It was named after Cayenne, the capital of French Guiana.

Constructed Response

The Guianas are two small nations and a colony on the north central Atlantic Ocean coast of South America. Give the former and current names of these two nations and the colony.

_____

_____

_____

_____

_____

_____

Name: _____   Date: _____

Map Follow-Up

Directions: Match the names listed below with the numbers on the map.

_____ Guyana   _____ French Guiana   _____ Suriname

_____ Atlantic Ocean   _____ Pacific Ocean   _____ Caribbean Sea

Nations of Guyana, French Guiana, and Suriname

South America's Islands: Close-Up

South America includes some of the world's most interesting islands.

The Archipelago
The **Archipelago** includes thousands of islands off the coast of Chile. Few people live there because of poor transportation and a lack of land that is suitable for farming.

The Galápagos Islands
- The **Galápagos Islands** are 600 miles (966 km) west of Ecuador. The Galápagos Island's capital is **Puerto Baquerizo Moreno.** The Galápagos Islands belong to Ecuador. There are nine larger and about 50 smaller islands. They are located directly on the equator.
- In 1835, Charles Darwin began his studies of the animals of the islands. He later wrote his famous book, *Origin of the Species,* based on some of his research while there.
- *Galápagos* is the Spanish word for tortoise. Some of the tortoises of the islands weigh more than 500 pounds (189 kg). Other interesting island animals are seals and four-foot-long iguanas. Rare birds living there include pelicans, penguins, flightless cormorants, and albatrosses. There are around 800 species of mollusks that have been identified in the Galápagos Islands. Eighteen percent of them are **endemic** (native to a particular country or area).
- The islands are now national parks and wildlife sanctuaries. Anyone wishing to visit Galápagos must have official permission.

Easter Island
- **Easter Island** is 2,350 miles (3,782 km) west of Chile. Chile annexed the island in 1888. Today, approximately 5,000 people live on the mysterious island.
- It is famous for more than 600 giant carved statues of people. The statues, called ***moai***, are carved from single blocks of black stone. They range from about 11 feet to 30 feet (3 m to 9 m) high. Historians do not know much about the people who carved the statues or why they carved them. It is estimated that the last of the statues was carved before 1400.

Trinidad and Tobago
- Trinidad and Tobago are two islands located off the northeast coast of Venezuela. They are usually considered to be part of the Caribbean islands even though they are close to South America. They now form an independent republic.
- Columbus visited Trinidad in 1498 during his third visit to the New World. Spanish and French settlers came during the 1500s. England controlled the islands from 1802 until 1962.
- Petroleum, natural gas, steel, and asphalt manufacturing have become the major industries.
- Both islands are known for a variety of colorful birds including egrets, herons, pink spoonbills, and scarlet ibises.

Name: _____ Date: _____

Knowledge Check

Matching

_____ 1. endemic

_____ 2. Puerto Baquerizo Moreno

_____ 3. Easter Island

_____ 4. Galápagos

_____ 5. moai

a. native to a particular country or area

b. Spanish word for tortoise

c. statues on Easter Island

d. mysterious island located 2,350 miles west of Chile

e. the Galápagos Island's capital

Multiple Choice

6. When did Columbus visit Trinidad?

   a. 1492

   b. 1802

   c. 1962

   d. 1498

7. Who wrote *Origin of the Species*?

   a. Columbus

   b. Charles Darwin

   c. Francisco Pizarro

   d. Galápagos

Did You Know?

In 1986, the government of Ecuador declared the Galápagos Islands a marine reserve.

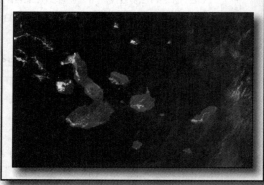

Constructed Response

Easter Island is described as mysterious. Explain why, using at least two details from the selection to support your answer.

_____

_____

_____

_____

_____

_____

_____

Glossary

Aconcagua - Western Hemisphere's highest point

agricultural - having to do with farming

agriculture processing - major industry of South America

Altiplano Plateau - a high plain in Bolivia where most of the people live

Amazon - South America's longest river

anaconda - world's largest snake

Andes Mountains - mountain system that runs down the length of the west coast of South America

Angel Falls - world's highest waterfall; in Venezuela

archipelago - an area of water with many scattered islands; the islands off Chile's west coast

Argentina - has most of South America's petroleum reserves

Asunción - Paraguay's capital and largest city

Atacama Desert - the world's driest place

Bogotá - Colombia's capital

Brasília - Brazil's capital city

Brazil - South America's largest and most populated country

Caracas - Venezuela's capital

Cayenne - capital of French Guiana

central valley - area in between mountain ranges down the middle of Chile where most of the people live

Chaco - name of the northern subtropical region of Argentina; mostly a forest region

colonial period - time when European nations ruled the colonies in South America; noted most for its architecture and religious art

Colombia - has the world's largest deposits of platinum

condor - South America's largest flying bird

conquistadors - Spanish soldiers

Continental Drift - Alfred Lothar Wegener's theory that the large landmass Pangaea had broken up and the continents were made of lighter rock that floated on top of heavier rock

Cuzco - capital of the Inca Empire

Easter Island - located 2,350 miles west of Chile; has statues called moai

endemic - native to a particular country or area

English - official language in Guyana

forests - cover over half of South America

Francisco Pizarro - led the Spanish invaders who conquered the Incas

Galápagos - Spanish word for tortoise

Galápagos Islands - located 600 miles west of Ecuador; declared a Marine Reserve in 1986

Georgetown - Guyana's capital

Gondwanaland - the name of the lower part of Pangaea when it divided into two continents during the Triassic Age

guitar - stringed instrument introduced by the Spanish

Guyana - means "land of many waters"

highland climate - climate in mountains and plateaus; the higher the altitude, the colder the temperatures

humid subtropical regions - also called savannas; rains most days in the summer; winter is the dry season

Incas - natives who first mined gold in the Andes Mountains and established an empire in the area that is now Peru

La Paz - Bolivia's capital

Laurasia - the name of the upper part of Pangaea when it divided into two continents during the Triassic Age

Lima - Peru's capital and largest city

Manco Capac - the first Inca, according to an Inca myth

maoi - stone statues on Easter Island

Mediterranean climate - warm and dry summers and mild and wet winters

mestizo - describes people descended from Native Americans and Spanish and Portuguese settlers

Montevideo - capital and largest city of Uruguay

Pablo Neruda - Noble Prize winning author

Pangaea - ancient landmass believed to have broken up to form today's continents

Pampas grassland - area in Argentina that contains some of the world's most fertile soil

Paramaribo - Suriname's capital

Patagonia - high plain in southern Argentina; cold, dry, windy, and sparsely populated

petroleum - one of the major sources of energy for South America

piranha - South American flesh-eating fish

Plate Tectonics - theory suggesting that Earth's plates move a few inches each year

Portuguese - official language of Brazil

Puerto Baquerizo Moreno - Galápagos Island's capital

quinoa - grown in the Andean highlands for its starchy seeds that are used as food and ground into flour

quipu - Inca knotted string invention used for counting

Quito - Ecuador's capital

rhea - South America's largest flightless bird

Roman Catholic - South America's largest religious group

São Paulo - Brazil's largest city

Santiago - Chile's capital and largest city

South America - fourth-largest continent

Spanish - official language of most of South America

spectacled bear - only type of bear native to South America

steppe - hot summers, cold winters, little rainfall

Suriname - Dutch Guiana was this country's name

tango - name of a popular dance from Argentina

Titicaca - world's highest navigable lake; on the border of Peru and Bolivia

tropical climate - hot temperatures and heavy rainfalls

Answer Keys

The Continents
Knowledge Check (p. 4)
Matching
1. c   2. d   3. e   4. a   5. b
Multiple Choice
6. b   7. a
Constructed Response
The earth's crust consists of 20 plates. Plate tectonics suggests that these plates move a few inches each year. Over time the plates have moved to their present positions.
Map Follow-Up (p. 5)
1. North America   2. South America
3. Europe   4. Africa
5. Antarctica   6. Asia
7. Australia   8. Arctic Ocean
9. Atlantic Ocean   10. Indian Ocean
11. Pacific Ocean

The Continent of South America
Knowledge Check (p. 9)
Matching
1. c   2. d   3. e   4. a   5. b
Multiple Choice
6. b   7. a
Constructed Response
These flatlands are used for farming and raising animal herds.
Map Follow-Up (p. 10)
1. Educator   2. Colombia   3. Venezuela
4. Guyana   5. Suriname   6. French Guiana
7. Peru   8. Brazil   9. Bolivia
10. Pacific Ocean 11. Chile   12. Paraguay
13. Argentina   14. Uruguay   15. Cape Horn
16. Atlantic Ocean
Map Follow-Up (p. 11)
1. Magdalena River   2. Orinoco River
3. Negro River   4. Amazon River
5. Madeira River   6. Tapajós River
7. Xingu River   8. Tocantins River
9. São Francisco River 10. Paraguay River
11. Paraná River   12. Lake Maracaibo
13. Lake Titicaca   14. Lake Poopó

South America's Climate
Knowledge Check (p. 14)
Matching
1. a   2. c   3. d   4. e   5. b
Multiple Choice
6. c   7. d

Constructed Response
The Mediterranean climate has warm, dry summers and mild, wet winters. A marine climate has milder summers than the Mediterranean climate and rainfall occurs year round.
Map Follow-Up (p. 15)
Teacher check climate map.

South America's Resources and Industries
Knowledge Check (p. 18)
Matching
1. d   2. e   3. b   4. c   5. a
Multiple Choice
6. b   7. a
Constructed Response
Many of the farmers in poorer regions raise just enough food for their own needs.
Map Follow-Up (p. 19)
Teacher check resources and industries map.

South America's Animal Life
Knowledge Check (p. 21)
Matching
1. b   2. c   3. e   4. d   5. a
Multiple Choice
6. a   7. d
Constructed Response
Llamas are important means of transporting materials on the steep slopes of the Andes Mountains. They also supply meat, milk, and wool to the natives.

The People of South America
Knowledge Check (p. 23)
Matching
1. d   2. e   3. a   4. c   5. b
Multiple Choice
6. d   7. b
Constructed Response
Spanish conquistadors conquered much of the continent. The conquistadors came in search of gold and other riches. They enslaved much of the native population and also brought slaves from Africa to work in the mines. Spanish is the official language of most of the continent.

The Inca Civilization
Knowledge Check (p. 25)
Matching
1. c   2. d   3. e   4. b   5. a
Multiple Choice
6. a   7. c

Constructed Response
The Incas developed terrace farming. They cut terraces into the steep sides of the mountains to create more farmland. They also dug irrigation systems to bring water from the mountain streams to the terraces.
Map Follow-Up (p. 26)
Teacher check Inca civilization map.

South American Culture
Knowledge Check (p. 28)
Matching
1. c   2. d   3. e   4. b   5. a
Multiple Choice
6. b   7. d
Constructed Response
The native civilizations used a variety of drums and flutes to accompany several festivals. The Europeans introduced stringed instruments to the continent. The guitar, introduced by the Spanish, became a favorite instrument.

Brazil, Paraguay, and Uruguay
Knowledge Check (p. 30)
Matching
1. c   2. d   3. b   4. e   5. a
Multiple Choice
6. c   7. c
Constructed Response
Flaxseed is an important crop used in the manufacture of ink, linseed oil, and paint.
Map Follow-Up (p. 31)
1. Atlantic Ocean   2. Brazil   3. Pacific Ocean
4. Paraguay   5. Uruguay   6. Cape Horn

Colombia, Ecuador, and Venezuela
Knowledge Check (p. 33)
Matching
1. e   2. a   3. d   4. b   5. c
Multiple Choice
6. c   7. b
Constructed Response
Miners have been extracting diamonds and iron ore for many years. Much of the iron ore was shipped to the United States to be made into steel.
Map Follow-Up (p. 34)
1. Atlantic Ocean   2. Venezuela
3. Colombia   4. Ecuador
5. Pacific Ocean   6. Caribbean Sea

Argentina, Chile, Peru, and Bolivia
Knowledge Check (p. 36)
Matching
1. d   2. c   3. a   4. b   5. e
Multiple Choice
6. c   7. c
Constructed Response
The northern part of Argentina is a subtropical region called the Chaco. It is mainly a forest region. The southern part of Argentina is a high plain named Patagonia. It is a cold, dry, windy, sparsely populated region.
Map Follow-Up (p. 37)
1. Atlantic Ocean   2. Peru   3. Bolivia
4. Chile   5. Pacific Ocean
6. Argentina   7. Cape Horn

Guyana, French Guiana, and Suriname
Knowledge Check (p. 39)
Matching
1. b   2. d   3. e   4. a   5. c
Multiple Choice
6. c   7. b
Constructed Response
The names are Guyana (formerly British Guiana), French Guiana, and Suriname (formerly Dutch Guiana).
Map Follow-Up (p. 40)
1. Guyana   2. Suriname
3. French Guiana   4. Atlantic Ocean
5. Pacific Ocean   6. Caribbean Sea

South America's Islands
Knowledge Check (p. 42)
Matching
1. a   2. e   3. d   4. b   5. c
Multiple Choice
6. d   7. b
Constructed Response
It is famous for more than 600 giant carved statues of people. The statues, called moai, are carved from single blocks of black stone. They range from about 11 feet to 30 feet. Not much is known about the people who carved the statues or why they carved them.

Bibliography

dividual Books:

Fowler, Allan. *South America.* Children's Press, 2001.

Kendall, Sarita. *The Incas.* (Worlds of the Past). Crestwood House, 1992.

Kramme, Michael. *Mayan, Incan, and Aztec Civilizations.* Mark Twain Media/Carson-Dellosa Publishing LLC, 2012.

Koponen, Libby. *South America.* Scholastic Library Publishing, 2009.

Reynolds, Jan. *Amazon Basin: Vanishing Cultures.* Lee & Low Books, 2007.

Schwartz, David. *Yanomami: People of the Amazon.* Lothrop Lee & Shepherd Books, 1995.

Shireman, Myrl. *South America.* Mark Twain Media/Carson-Dellosa Publishing Co., Inc., 1998.

Waterlow, Julia. *The Amazon.* Heinemann Library, 1993.

Specific Countries (series):

Cultures of the World (Series published by Benchmark Books/Marshall Cavendish). Each book was published between 2002 and 2011, contains 144 pages. Countries included: *Argentina, Bolivia, Chile, Colombia, Ecuador, Paraguay, Peru, Suriname, Trinidad and Tobago,* and *Venezuela.*

Major World Nations (Series published by Chelsea House). Each book was published between 1997 and 2001, contains 88 to 128 pages. Countries included: *Argentina, Bolivia, Brazil, Chile, Colombia, Ecuador, Guyana, Paraguay, Peru, Suriname, Trinidad and Tobago, Uruguay,* and *Venezuela.*

Enchantment of the World (Second Series published by Children's Press). Each book was published between 1998 and 2009, contains 144 pages. Countries included: *Argentina, Bolivia, Brazil, Chile, Colombia, Ecuador, Guiana, Paraguay, Peru, Suriname, Uruguay,* and *Venezuela.*